God Is More than Enough

LIFECHANGE BOOKS

GOD is more than ENOUGH

TONY EVANS

Multnomah® Publishers *Sisters, Oregon*

GOD IS MORE THAN ENOUGH
published by Multnomah Publishers, Inc.

© 2004 by Tony Evans
International Standard Book Number: 1-59052-337-7

Cover image by Getty Images/Ruth Sorenson

Unless otherwise indicated, Scripture quotations are from:
The Holy Bible, New King James Version © 1984 by Thomas Nelson, Inc.
Other Scripture quotations are from:
The Holy Bible, New International Version (NIV) © 1973, 1984 by International Bible Society,
used by permission of Zondervan Publishing House
New American Standard Bible (NASB) © 1960, 1977 by the Lockman Foundation

Multnomah is a trademark of Multnomah Publishers, Inc.,
and is registered in the U.S. Patent and Trademark Office.
The colophon is a trademark of Multnomah Publishers, Inc.

Printed in the United States of America

For information:
MULTNOMAH PUBLISHERS, INC. • P. O. BOX 1720 • SISTERS, OR 97759

Library of Congress Cataloging-in-Publication Data

Evans, Anthony T.
    God is more than enough / by Tony Evans.
        p. cm.
    ISBN 1-59052-337-7 (Hardcover)
    1. Bible O.T. Psalms XXIII--Criticism, interpretation, etc. 2. God—Biblical teaching.
    3. Christian life—Biblical teaching. I. Title.

    BS145023rd .E93 2004
    223'.206—dc22

                                                            2003023593

04 05 06 07 08—10 9 8 7 6 5 4 3 2 1 0

Contents

INTRODUCTION
The Attack 7

CHAPTER ONE
The Basic Question
Just Who Is Your Shepherd? 11

CHAPTER TWO
God Is More than Enough…
to Meet Your Spiritual Needs 27

CHAPTER THREE
God Is More than Enough…
to Meet Your Directional Needs 39

CHAPTER FOUR
God Is More than Enough…
to Meet Your Emotional Needs 51

CHAPTER FIVE
God Is More than Enough…
to Meet Your Physical Needs 65

CHAPTER SIX
God Is More than Enough…
to Meet Your Eternal Needs 79

THE ATTACK

There is not a single need you could possibly have that isn't addressed by the words of Psalm 23.

Not one.

No matter what inadequacy or hardship you're facing and how deeply you're facing it, no matter how problematic or distressful or exacting it may be—if the Lord is your Shepherd, He can meet all of your needs. The Twenty-third Psalm was David's way of saying God is more than enough to meet whatever lack or constraint or extremity or impossibility you might ever encounter.

And that's why, although this immortal psalm is one of the most evocative and poetic passages ever written either inside the Bible or out, it is so much more than a sweet-sounding set of verses to console your heart in tough times. It is magnificent and enrapturing as a literary masterpiece, yet its depth goes far beyond.

Beautiful as it is, this psalm is an *attack*.

It's an attack on our debilitating lack of trust in God and the great trauma of insecurity that's brought on by such doubts and disbelief. Most Christians do not actually believe that God is more than enough. Too often, God is the last one that we appeal to. And so we wind up becoming spiritually emaciated, unable to handle the ups and downs of life.

This profound psalm is an attack on our chronic inclination to look for fulfillment in all the wrong places. So many Christians are living lives of profound dissatisfaction. We go hungrily from one table to the next, experiencing one disappointment after another, and we're *just not satisfied*. We all discover, once we've lived long enough, that there's no friendship, no relationship, no ownership, no championship, no scholarship, no fellowship that can fully satisfy our wants. Psalm 23, however, offers us a vastly different approach to the question of satisfaction in life. At the heart of it we find what we could call, in popular terms, the secret to a happy life.

Furthermore, this psalm is an attack on our very serious sin of self-sufficiency—the stubborn independence that makes us determined to deal with our own needs in our own way. Of all the sins a person can commit, at the top of the list is self-sufficiency, for it is fundamentally the sin of pride. It's thinking, *I can function independently of God; I'm all I need to take care of myself.* But what we're actually able to do for ourselves is utterly infinitesimal compared to what God can do for us, and that's why He designed us to live in utter dependence on Him. So the result of our foolish self-focus is that we narrow our existence to an uncomfortably restricted dimension.

Years ago I took my children on a certain attraction at Walt Disney World. As our floating vessel cruised along a winding stream, we were taken alongside elaborately staged representations of different cultures with different children dressed in different ways, all of them singing the same song in different languages: "It's a small world after all, it's a small world after all…"

The first time I heard the song, it was okay. The second time was tolerable. The third time, it started getting on my nerves. On the fourth time through I wanted to jump in the water and swim out of there! This small world, being endlessly sung about by small people, was becoming acutely irritating.

We're each of us so small, after all, and the world of our own resources is so pitifully insufficient. When you try living within those confines it can only mean a cramped existence, and eventually you can't help wanting something more. You're like a plane circling in a holding pattern—every time you look down, the ground looks oh so familiar, and you want something else, somewhere new, something more. You can't help wanting to break out and see what's different and wider and better, to see life unfold as you believe it ought to, as you so deeply desire it to.

That's God's desire for you as well, and the kind of relationship with Him that Psalm 23 portrays is the pathway to get you there.

As we move, alertly and reflectively, through this tender psalm, you'll soon see that my driving message in this book is simple, not deep; you don't have to be a theologian or a Bible scholar or have a set of commentaries nearby to quickly understand where I'm headed. The good news of the Twenty-third Psalm boils down to one essential point: *If the Lord is your Shepherd, He will meet all your needs.* By allowing Him to freely do this for us, we can rest assured that whatever possible need arises, our Good Shepherd is sure to be there.

Chapter One

THE BASIC QUESTION

Just Who Is Your Shepherd?

Right there in the opening line of Psalm 23, we find the essence and climax and consummation of what the whole psalm is about: "The LORD is my shepherd; I shall not want."

But immediately a problem reveals itself in our reaction to these well-known words from David. While everybody likes part two of the verse—naturally we want our wants and needs provided for—many of us would just as soon skip part one, the bothersome part about making the Lord our Shepherd.

So my simple question for you is this: I'm assuming the

Lord is your Savior, but is He also your Shepherd? In other words, do you want the promise of the second half of verse 1 bad enough to get the first half right?

I assure you that you'll be better prepared to answer that question after we take a closer look at each word in this brief opening phrase of this most famous psalm and we experience the deep and true encouragement to be found there.

"THE LORD..."

First of all, David identifies his Shepherd as "the Lord." What does David really mean by that name?

The Hebrew word for "Lord" in this verse is *Yahweh*. That's God's formal name, and it takes us back to Exodus 3, where God was leading Moses into a tough situation that was too big for him to handle. On that occasion, God revealed to Moses that His name is "I Am That I Am." That's *Yahweh*, the same "Lord" that David talks about.

What kind of name is this? If Yahweh the Lord is the one who meets all our needs, we really do need to know and understand His name.

"I Am That I Am" conveys first of all God's *self-existence*. He's the eternally existent One. God exists because God exists. He isn't defined by anything outside Himself.

His existence is wrapped up in His existence; the total circumference of who God is within God Himself.

Therefore God is also *self-sufficient*. He depends on nothing outside Himself in order to be God. He is sustained by Himself, which means He is of necessity consistent with Himself.

When I'm cold, I need a coat. When I'm hungry, I need food. When I'm sick, I need a doctor. I have to go outside myself to have my needs met. But not God, because all that He requires, He is. What this means practically is that God has what no one in all creation has: an eternally unchangeable nature. God will always be as He is now and as He reveals Himself to be, because "I Am That I Am." God is the same yesterday and today and tomorrow. His essential nature does not change because it *cannot* change, because it's defined by His own internal reality that needs nothing outside Himself.

You and I, on the other hand, live in an atmosphere of constant change. The weather changes, our health changes, our mood changes, our level of knowledge changes. We constantly fluctuate and oscillate and deviate as we find ourselves in varying circumstances.

But God never changes. What He was, He is. What He is, He will always be.

That means God is the most consistent thing in your

life. The most dependable thing you have going for you is not your family or your friends or your bank account or your life's work. The best and the most consistent thing you have going for you is your God, and we see that even in His name. "I Am That I Am," He says. There is constancy with God.

When you're in trouble, where do you go first?

When it came to meeting his needs and overcoming his struggles in life, David knew he needed someone consistent and steadfast to lean on. He didn't want a Shepherd who would only be there sometimes. He needed a Shepherd he could bank on 24/7. And only the Lord God can be that.

And because of who He is, God already possesses all that it takes to fully satisfy us. All the raw materials necessary to address our deepest needs are already built into His identity. He doesn't have to go look for it or buy it or borrow it. He *has* it, because I Am That I Am. He's a one-stop shop.

So you want to make sure your Shepherd is not some cheap god, but the unchanging Yahweh, the Lord, the only God. The Bible is His résumé, and it's a thick one. He's got all the qualifications, all the capacity required to handle the job. He's managing the lives of billions of people all at the same time. And while He's taking care of that, He keeps the earth's rivers flowing and the breezes blowing and the fields and the flowers and the trees all growing. Meanwhile, He keeps our planet rotating on its axis and revolving around the sun, even as he manages the affairs of stars and galaxies that only He can ever know the number of.

That's why David tells the Lord, *"You* are my shepherd; I'm looking only to *You."*

Is the Lord your Shepherd, too? It's easy to answer yes, but how do you know if it's something real for you or if you're just saying the words?

Let me give you a simple test. When you're challenged or tested or stretched, when you need help, where do you go first? Where do you look? Who do you turn to first? Most folks go to God only after they've tried everything else—when nothing else is working, *then* they try praying.

Think about your last crisis. Whatever or whoever you went to first for help in that crisis, *that* is your shepherd.

A man on a trip into the African rainforest was following a guide. As they pushed onward into deeper and darker jungle, the guide with his machete was whacking away at the thick green growth that rose like a wall everywhere before them.

"How do you know where to go?" the man asked. "Where's the path?"

The guide replied, *"I am the path."*

It's a jungle out there, and we need a guide who knows where he's going and what he's doing. God is that guide, because He is the great I Am.

"...Is..."

David didn't say, "The Lord *was* my shepherd." He didn't say, "The Lord *will be* my shepherd." He said, "The Lord *is* my shepherd." Right now. In this very moment. It's a present-tense relationship, which it must be, since God's name is I Am, and that name also reveals His *eternal* nature.

When God says, "I Am That I Am," He's saying, "I am always in the present tense." Everything for God is *now*. God has never experienced a yesterday. Nor does He have a tomorrow, so God never has to use the words *I hope...*

Why is it important to know this about God? Because when I have a need, my need is in the *now*. When I have a struggle, my struggle is in the *now*. When I have a hurt, my hurt is in the *now*. And God tells us, "I am the Eternal Now. I can meet you in your present experience."

Then there are those of us that are worried and upset and even popping pills because we're thinking about *tomorrow*. But God shepherds us one day at a time—He makes sure we have enough grace to cover the troubles of today.

God says, "Don't worry. When you get to tomorrow, I'll be there. Just deal with today. Just let Me be your Shepherd, and I will take care of you. Receive My grace for this moment. And if you take time to thank Me for the present, you won't have time to worry about tomorrow."

God meets today's needs today. He'll meet tomorrow's needs tomorrow.

When the people of Israel journeyed through the wilderness, God rained down a certain food for them every morning from on high, like cornflakes from the sky, and the people gathered it up from the ground for that day's sustenance. He gave them each morning only a day's supply of these flakes, except on the sixth day of the week, when He gave them twice as much so they could rest on the Sabbath and not have to gather their food.

It was always enough, but *only* enough, to supply each day's need.

God wanted His people to recognize Him as their *daily* provider. He wanted them to *constantly* look to Him for their provision.

That's why God isn't satisfied with our go-to-church-on-Sunday-and-I'm-good-for-the-week approach to the Christian life. Once you hit Monday, Sunday's over. It's "was," not "is." God wants a moment-by-moment, day-by-day relationship with each of us, not a once-a-week "refresher."

"...My..."

"The Lord is *my* shepherd." This is an individual situation, a personal relationship. It wasn't enough for David that the Lord is *a* shepherd or even *the* Shepherd. He knew he had to be able to say that the great I Am is *my* Shepherd, to say that the Lord is the one I'm depending on for *my* needs and *my* salvation.

Sometimes at a crowded restaurant, when you're waiting for a table and your name is on the waiting list, the hostess will give you a pager to hold. When it's time for you and your party to be seated, the pager will vibrate. The restaurant staff has your name, and they're preparing a table just for you. And once it's ready, if you're still patiently waiting and holding on to that pager, it will let you know.

Now some people wonder why their spirituality is so lifeless and nothing's vibrating. It's because they're not holding on to God's pager and patiently seeking and awaiting their Shepherd's personal instructions just for them. So they miss the table He's prepared for them.

I have shirts that are monogrammed with the letters *T. E.* They're not just off-the-rack shirts; they're personalized. A lot of Christians want an off-the-rack God, but what God wants with us is a monogrammed relationship. He has your initials inscribed on His heart—and He want His Son's initials inscribed on yours.

God gave you a unique personality, a unique orientation, a unique purpose, a unique calling. And He has to be your personal Shepherd in order for you to know His unique will for you. He wants a relationship with you that's unlike what He has with anybody else.

You may think I'm going too far by saying that, but if you read in Revelation, in Christ's messages to the seven churches, you will find this promise regarding the believer who's committed to Him:

> "And I will give him a white stone, and on the stone a new name written which no one knows except him who receives it."
>
> REVELATION 2:17

The Lord is saying, "I will give you a private name that only the two of us know." God is going to monogram you, to mark the most intimately personal relationship possible. And He's nurturing that relationship with you even now.

Some things, of course, apply equally to each and every Christian. The promises and commands and standards of Scripture are for us all. But just like your fingerprints are unique and different, so also is God's interaction with you unique and different, because *you* are unique and different. And that's why you need to learn to hear God's voice to know when He's speaking specifically to you, and how He's particularly leading you in the application (or the *illumination*—that's the theological word) of the Scriptures to your life.

"...SHEPHERD."

"The Lord is my *shepherd.*" A shepherd's job is to look after the comprehensive well-being of the sheep. And for that job, there's certainly nothing better than someone who can actually meet those comprehensive needs.

In Jeremiah 23:4, God describes the role of a shepherd as one who feeds his flock in such a way that "they shall fear no more, nor be dismayed, nor shall they be lacking." In Ezekiel 34:2–4, God lists all that He expects a shepherd to do: feed the flock, strengthen the weak, heal the sick, bind up the broken, bring back the strays, seek the lost.

That's what being a shepherd means to God.

And there's more: "The good shepherd *gives His life* for the sheep" (John 10:11). The superior shepherd is willing to make the ultimate sacrifice—he puts it all on the line for the sheep.

And so when selecting a shepherd for your own life, the proof of a good one is whether that shepherd has given his life for you. And you have that proof. *This is exactly what*

Jesus has done for you. You know He loves you as no one else possibly can.

But in order for Him to be your Shepherd, you must first recognize yourself as a sheep. Shepherds don't tend wolves or dogs; shepherds shepherd sheep. And if you don't think of yourself as a sheep, you're not qualified to receive Him as your Shepherd.

That's why many of us aren't see-ing God meet our needs. We haven't decided yet that we are sheep. We resist what that implies. We resist it because fully recognizing yourself as a sheep will mean humbling yourself and identifying with a sheep in at least three ways.

Do you think of yourself as a sheep?

First of all, sheep are *dumb.* Have you ever been to the circus and seen sheep performing to the commands of a sheep trainer? Have you ever seen a farmer teach his sheep to do tricks? No, because sheep are too dumb. And to ask the Lord to be your Shepherd means realizing and admitting how limited your intelligence really is.

We've all said to ourselves, *How could I be so stupid?* Because sheep are dumb, they regularly wander and stray. Stupid as they are, they regularly think they know best what to do and where to go. Isaiah 53:6 says, "We all, like sheep, have gone astray, each of us has turned to his own way" (NIV). What does that say about us? That we're dumb.

Second, sheep are *defenseless.* They have no fangs, no stingers, no claws, and they don't gallop or fly or swim. That's why we don't have professional sports teams named after them—no such thing as the Dallas Sheep, the Chicago Sheep, the San Francisco Sheep. That's also why we don't use sheep for protection; we don't have guard sheep. You never hear anyone shout, "Sic 'em, sheep!" Sheep need protection themselves, or else they get eaten up by an animal that is armed with fangs. To want the Lord as your Shepherd means realizing how vulnerable you are.

Finally, sheep are also *dirty.* Cats and birds and most other animals will clean themselves, but sheep will stay dirty forever unless the shepherd gives them a bath. And to have the Lord as your Shepherd means being willing to admit you need Him to wash you and make you clean.

Unless you understand that you have these limitations and undesirable traits, you'll never recognize your comprehensive and constant need for a Shepherd. You'll want a Shepherd for emergencies only.

But if you accept the truth as David did, then you can call the Lord Himself your Shepherd. For even though we're dumb, defenseless, dirty sheep, God still takes care of us because we're *His* sheep. And the beauty of a Good Shepherd is, he's so knowledgeable about our foolishness and our frailty and our filthiness that He knows exactly how to address all of it, even when we hardly begin to recognize what's wrong with us.

GOD'S FULL SERVICE

There are two ways to get gasoline for your car.

In the first method, you pull up to the self-service pump. You get out of your car, open the tiny door that covers the gas tank, and unscrew the gas cap. You turn to the pump and slip your credit card in the slot and punch the appropriate buttons. You take the nozzle from the pump and insert it into your tank.

You stand there until the nozzle clicks, and then you click some more to squeeze in all the gasoline you can. You put the nozzle away, screw on your gas cap, and close the tiny door. Then you open your car door, get in, and drive off.

Now if the weather is cold, you get cold while doing all this. If the weather's hot, you get hot. If it's raining, you get wet. But at least you're able to say, "I did it myself."

But there's another way to get gasoline. You drive up to the full-service pumps, and you remain comfortably seated.

Someone comes out to you, takes your credit card, and runs it through the slot for you. He opens the little door back there, unscrews the gas cap, and inserts the nozzle for you. And while it's filling up, he washes your front windows and your side windows. If you ask, he'll even check the air in your tires. He'll lift the hood and check your oil. And when the gas nozzle clicks, he'll take it out, screw the cap back on, and close the little door for you. And after all of that, he'll thank *you* for using their services.

Why do we insist on living self-service lives?

Meanwhile, the wind hasn't messed up your hair, and you don't have the smell of gasoline on your hands. It may be cold outside, but you're still warm in your car. If it's raining, you're still dry. If it's hot outside, you're still cool. All because there was somebody at the station whose job it was to provide you full service.

The reason so many of us cannot sincerely pray, "The Lord is my shepherd; I shall not want," is that we're still living self-service lives. We're saying, "I'm going to pull it off. I'm going to make it happen. I'm going to cut the deal. I'm going to reverse this situation." And we get out and try it, and we wind up all sweaty and sore and dirty and frustrated.

But God is running a full-service station. And if you'll just pull up and rest, He'll come out and not only do what you came for, but He'll take care of some stuff you never asked for—clean your dirty windows, check for low oil. He's going to take care of *all* of your needs.

It all comes down to this: If the Lord is your Shepherd, if you will be His sheep, He'll take care of everything—your spiritual needs, your directional needs, your emotional needs, your physical needs, your eternal needs. He'll satisfy them all.

And all His sheep say, "Amen."

Chapter Two

GOD IS MORE
THAN ENOUGH...

to Meet Your Spiritual Needs

If the Lord is your Shepherd, He will meet your *spiritual* need.

David says,

> He makes me to lie down in green pastures;
> He leads me beside the still waters.
> He restores my soul.

VV. 2–3

David's first message in this psalm is especially for those of you who are spiritually tired, spiritually drained. Your spiritual resources have ebbed. You've been waiting patiently for God, and He's taking too long.

It's as if you've telephoned, but somebody pushed the "hold" button on your life and then forgot about you. Or you've been in the waiting room, waiting and waiting for your name to be called, but without a single indication that it ever will be. Or you're at a stoplight and the light won't change.

Like a tire going flat, all your spiritual air has been released. You're spiritually discouraged because you can't find God. Oh, you know He's there; you're too scared not to believe that. But He seems such a long distance off, and dryness of soul has set in.

David knows what you're talking about, because he's been there. The David who says, "The Lord is my shepherd," is the same David who cries out, "My soul thirsts for You; my flesh longs for You in a dry and thirsty land where there is no water" (Psalm 63:1).

It's in the midst of such a wilderness that your Shepherd shows up. It's in the midst of your spiritual discouragement, disgust, defeat, struggle, wrestling, failure, futility, emptiness, agony, anger, agitation—when you want to scream out for God's presence or even scream out against

Him—in the midst of all this, David says, if the Lord is your Shepherd, He'll meet you at the place of your spiritual need.

One reason we have such intense spiritual need is that our own sin drains us. Another reason is the unavoidable reality of our environment. We've all received mail addressed simply to "Occupant"; sometimes we lose spiritual resources merely because we're an occupant of planet earth. It isn't because of anything we did wrong, but just because we happen to live here.

The unavoidable reality of our environment drains us.

The combination of the world, the flesh, and the devil can suck out your spiritual vitality. In the midst of that weariness and lethargy, when you run out of spiritual gas and you're making it only on the fumes, you try to pray, and no words come. You know you ought to be reading your Bible, but the letters on the page all run together, and none of it makes sense. You don't want to hear another sermon or another Christian radio program or another gospel song. You don't want to hear from spiritual people, especially when you suspect they must be faking their positive outlooks.

You're only going through the spiritual motions. You're

nodding, you're saying "Amen," your head is raised, but deep down in your soul, you're running on empty.

You've lost your spiritual fire. And that's the perfect point, the ideal point, to discover that God is your Shepherd.

TO THE PLACE OF REFRESHMENT

It's at this point that David reminds us, "He makes me to lie down in green pastures." God doesn't *ask* me to lie down; He *makes* me.

And He makes me lie down not just in any old pasture, but in *green* pastures—that's the emphasis in that phrase. God makes sure the pastures are lush and green. Likewise in the next phrase: "He leads me beside the *still* waters." Not just any stream, but waters of quietness.

David kept sheep in the hills of Judah. I've been in that country in the summertime, and it's blazing hot with the sun beating down. You don't have to be out there long before it sucks the energy out of you. But a good shepherd will take his sheep from the barren, sun-exposed heights, where there's no life, to a shaded place where there's a green carpet of grass in which they can lie in comfort, and where the breeze blowing off the still waters is cool and refreshing.

In other words, the shepherd renews them...*restores*

them. But to do this he first has to force the sheep to lie down there, or else they would keep wandering, trying to make their own way.

FORCED DOWN

As long as you're self-sufficient, as long as you think you can fix your problems on your own, you'll only find yourself becoming more spiritually drained. God has to make you lie down—He has to put you in a situation you can't get out of. He forces the scenario where every door you try is locked. Everything you fix breaks again. You fall flat on your face.

To lie down means you have to get *low*. You know when you've been made to lie down, because you're desperate. And when you're desperate, when you're on your last leg, ready to throw in the towel, you're in a great position for the Shepherd.

God puts you in circumstances that rob you of your independence and cause you to be totally dependent, so you have to rest on Him. You finally realize that if *God* doesn't renew you, you won't get renewed; if

When we look up, He's all we're seeing.

He doesn't empower you, you won't get empowered; if *He* doesn't release you, you'll forever be in bondage.

God is trying to force us into a place of total abandonment to Him. He wants to bring you and me to the end of ourselves, so that when we look up, He's all we're seeing. But for some of us, it takes a long time before we're willing to let this process happen. So God keeps creating situations and allowing scenarios and causing issues we don't like, and He won't get rid of them until you understand that you're totally, absolutely dependent on Him.

FLAT ON YOUR BACK

I heard about a huge loggerhead turtle that laid her eggs on a Florida beach and then became disoriented. Instead of returning back toward the sea, she began walking farther into the sand dunes, where she was discovered by a park ranger. The ranger took a crowbar and flipped her over upon her back. Then he used chains to connect the turtle's legs to the tow bar on his jeep, and he towed the turtle back toward the sea and turned her loose.

While that turtle was being dragged along, I'm sure she didn't consider it a comfortable situation. We often feel the same way about what God is doing to us. Sometimes He has to turn our life upside down, and while we're on our back getting dragged, it's hard to know whether we're being killed or saved.

Sometimes you don't know whether God is delivering you or doing you in. But He has put you in a place where there's room for only one God—and it isn't you.

HE GIVES YOU BACK YOUR SOUL

All this is because God has a purpose.

And what's His goal? What is God's reason for the crises He creates in our lives that force us to lie down?

David tells us: "He restores my soul." God wants to give you back your soul.

Your soul is who you are, your personhood, your identity. I'm not you, and you're not me, not because our body structures are different but because we have different souls. The soul is the "you." And when you become confused about who you are, and you lose your sense of well-being, your sense of purpose, your sense of direction, your sense of hope—then your soul needs restoring.

That process takes time. It's like making your cell phone lie down in the recharger after you've used it and talked on it all day. You make it lie down so it can get new energy, new strength. If you don't, it may not work for you tomorrow.

And the restoration process often must begin with pain. Antique furniture is restored only after the sanding process is finished, and so it is with us. The sanding process is painful, but oh, the restoration looks magnificent!

It's like making a wrinkled shirt lie down on the ironing board, then you apply the hot iron and steam to that shirt, and the heat takes out the wrinkles. It takes heat to get out the stuff that doesn't belong there. Only then does the shirt look good and you're ready to wear it. God wants you to look good on Him, but He must make you lie down so He can apply the fire to your life and smooth out the wrinkles.

WE ALL NEED IT

There's not a Christian you know who hasn't needed a restored soul. There's not a person in your church who hasn't run dry spiritually at times, and been wrung out, and felt that it's not worth it, that it's too tough. Every believer you know has at some point been ready to throw in the towel.

David doesn't say that if the Lord is your Shepherd, you'll never need a restored soul. Rather, he shows us that if the Lord is your Shepherd, He'll restore your soul when you need it, even if He has to make you lie down, even if He has to create a scenario to force you to recognize your dependence upon Him, and He is then free to renew you spiritually. The Lord can do that, the Lord wants to do that, and the Lord will do that for His sheep.

He puts you in a rest mode—still waters, green pastures. It may take trials to get you there. It may take struggles to get you there. It may take successes to get you there. But whatever it takes, it becomes clear that you can't get there on your own.

In that position He restores or gives you back a renewed sense of hope, a renewed sense of purpose, a renewed sense of being. He gives you back your life.

AFRAID TO LIE DOWN

One of the ways I paid my way through my first year of seminary was by being a lifeguard and water safety instructor. I taught people how to swim, and I developed a pretty good routine for doing it.

Nonswimmers are often afraid of the water, so you have to get them acclimated to it—you splash a little water on them, then you get them to put their head down in the water. Then comes the big one: They lay out on the water and float.

Getting splashed was only a little irritating for them at worst, and putting their head in the water wasn't really so difficult as long as they could feel their feet firmly planted on the bottom of the pool. But lying flat on the water, with nothing else beneath them, and with no control—now that was often a problem. They were thinking, *What if I go under?*

So I stretched out my arms in the water beneath them, and I assured them, "You'll be in my arms; I'll hold you up." Then they could feel secure to lie down on the insecurity of water.

A lot of us are scared to lie down; we wonder how we'll ever make it if we're no longer in control. God is telling us we won't learn how to swim in this life until we're no longer in control, until we understand that it's His arms, and not our ability, that holds us up. He tells us, "I am your ability. I am your sufficiency. I am your surplus. I am your Shepherd, and I'll meet your needs even when you're drained of life."

For Something New

When God lets everything collapse on you, it's because He's getting ready to do something new with you. When God allows things to be destroyed around you, it's because He's preparing to build something. When He implodes your life, it's because He's ready for a new structure to go up. He wants you to rise up with a new soul, a new insight, a new you. He wants to spiritually rejuvenate you.

We're like a baby with a soiled diaper, and the mother who cleans the mess and changes the diaper is like the Lord, our Shepherd. As messy as we are, that doesn't turn Him away, because the Shepherd loves his sheep. God in His grace will make you lie down, pull out His wipes of grace, clean you up, powder you down, then lotion you up...and then it will be time to play again, because that's what grace does. Grace gives people back their souls, clean and fresh.

Maybe you're in the checkout line at this moment—you're almost ready to check out on God, to check out on the church, to check out on your faith. You're tired of trying, too discouraged to keep going. But before you give it all up, understand what David is saying.

God has you in this place because He's making you lie down. He has you flat on your back so you can tell Him, "I need you as I've never needed You before." God has caused you to lie down in green pastures, and led you by still waters, because there's a delivery coming on. And the delivery will restore your soul.

So don't check out just yet. Relinquish your self-sufficiency, your self-dependence. Say to Him, "Here I am, Lord." And get ready to see what your good Shepherd will do for you....

Chapter Three

GOD IS MORE
THAN ENOUGH...

to Meet Your Directional Needs

Having made you lie down in order to restore your soul and give you back your life, God now wants to guide your path...so you can say together with David,

> He leads me in the paths of righteousness
> For His name's sake.

v. 3

If the Lord is your Shepherd, He can meet not only your spiritual needs, but also your directional needs. His goal is to begin the process of spiritual direction, to become your spiritual tour guide.

Life is full of choices, full of decisions, full of options. If we could turn back the hands of time, most of us would change some of our past choices because they've resulted in finding ourselves on the path of wrongness, not righteousness. Sheep, too, are known to wander, to veer off the path. All you need for a sheep to wander is a good-looking trail through some bushes with berries. The sheep will gravitate to the appeal of the berries, even at the expense of moving away from the shepherd.

Sheep feel they're self-sufficient until they get in trouble, which again shows how dumb sheep are. They think they know the correct path when they actually have no clue. You and I tend to have that same strong sense of self-sufficiency, but if the truth be told, there are so many things in life where we just have to say, "I don't know what to do." We don't have an answer, we don't have a solution, we don't have a direction.

FIRST, THE RESTING

Have you ever been walking somewhere and become disoriented, then started walking faster? Sometimes we think speeding up will clarify direction. But speeding up, when you don't know where you're going, only gets you more lost—quicker.

Don't fail to notice in Psalm 23 that verse 2 comes before verse 3—the right pathways come only after the resting. If you're going to let God lead you, if you're going to hear the Spirit speak to your heart, you need to be in a rest mode, not a rush mode. God wants to guide our path, but He can guide us only if we're able to hear Him.

It's hard for me to rest. I tend to think I'm sinning if I'm not busy, if I'm not working myself as well as creating more work for others. But David shows us that it's in this green-pasture position, this still-water place, this rest mode and sense of dependence, that God guides us forward where He wants us to go. That's when we're in position for God to talk to us.

You need to be in a rest mode, not a rush mode.

This was David's secret. He knew how to become quiet before God. He spent a lot of time meditating. He said to the Lord, "I meditate on You in the night watches" (Psalm 63:6) and "I meditate on all Your works; I muse on the work of Your hands. I spread out my hands to You; my soul longs for You like a thirsty land" (143:5–6). And he prayed that the meditation of his heart would be acceptable in God's sight (Psalm 19:14). David would find a place of solitude without distraction, and there he would focus his mind and heart on God, knowing that God would speak back to him.

Most people seek to determine God's leading only from their circumstances. But our circumstances never *determine* the leading of God; they only *confirm* God's leading. The same is true for counsel from other people. They can confirm God's leading—"in the multitude of counselors there is safety" (Proverbs 11:14)—but people cannot definitively resolve for us the leading of God. Sometimes God will lead you in a way where every outward circumstance looks the opposite of what He's told you, or when hardly a single person seems to understand what you're doing, but you know you heard from God.

All this is because God's leading happens in the heart. It happens in that rest, that place of quietness, where He can lead you and guide you and direct you.

FAITH IGNITED

But does God still speak in that way to people today? Absolutely. He does it in two ways: He speaks objectively through His Word, and subjectively through His Spirit. We're to read the Bible and hear God's voice there, and then live in His presence and experience how He takes those truths from the pages of the Book and writes them on the heart, just as His New Covenant promises.

There's a tension today between a Christianity you can understand and a Christianity you can feel, or between the academic (or intellectual) side and the experiential side. One group says God wants to sanctify your mind and make it full of truth. But their hearts can seem as dead as a door-knob—no passion and no fire. Some of the meanest Christians I've met know their Bible. They're irritating and aggravating, but they quote verses, and never miss Bible study, and they're there every time the church door opens.

On the other side are the feely-feely Christians. They may be doing something that goes against the Bible, and the Spirit is telling them to stop, but they're feeling good and they're excited about it, so they keep on.

A truly intelligent faith sets fire to the soul.

There's no legitimate battle between an intellectual faith and a passionate faith. A truly intelligent faith sets fire to the soul; it is objective truth resulting in passionate expression. Nobody wants a love they can't feel. Nobody wants a love that doesn't set them on fire.

When the Holy Spirit showed up in the book of Acts to lead God's people, it says there were "tongues of fire"; there was passion; there were flames. God wants a faith full of fire—not just a raging wildfire, but intelligent fire, fire in its rightful place, fire that comes from God's truth and that burns in the soul as well as the mind.

That's one of the ways you sense your calling. It's a fire you can't put out. As Jeremiah said, "His word was in my heart like a burning fire shut up in my bones; I was weary of holding it back, and I could not" (Jeremiah 20:9). You'll know you're hearing from God when the power of His Word penetrates deep into the inner resources of your being, deep into your spirit. It's when God's objective Word is combined with the subjective spiritual reality of the Holy Spirit communicating to your human spirit. When those two connect, you just had a conversation with God.

God didn't save you simply to give you a doctrinal knowledge of him. Now don't get me wrong. Doctrine is critical because doctrine is foundational. But doctrine only gives you information about God. It does not give you interaction with God. Interaction with God is the role of the Holy Spirit.

We discover in 1 Corinthians 2:12 that we have received God's Holy Spirit "that we might know the things that have been freely given to us by God." God has guidance He wants to give you for free through the Spirit. And the Holy Spirit knows God's signals, because "the Spirit searches all things, yes, the deep things of God" (1 Corinthians 2:10). Think of the Holy Spirit as a deep-sea diver, going down to the depths of things that only God could know, only God could do, only God could experience. And Paul tells us that God reveals those very things unto us into our experience.

THE RIGHT WAY

So God is our consummate guide. And where He leads us is always in paths of righteousness. God guides us that we might arrive at an appointed destination, and that appointed destination is always His righteous will. Righteousness is the *right* way, and the Good Shepherd knows the right way.

We need to be led in the path that's right because we spend so much time in the path that's wrong. And we're on the wrong path so much because we live by our own understanding, our own ideas. Of course God wants you to use the brain He's given you and the resources He's given

The Holy Spirit wants to take you beyond your limits.

you, but you can only go so far with your own human ability. You're always limited in your natural self. But the Holy Spirit wants to take you beyond those limits.

If you feel to some extent that you're a lost sheep, then stop where you are—don't move, don't keep wandering, and your Shepherd will find you. He'll locate you and show you the right way.

You say, "But my situation is dark." But God knows the right way, and He'll show it to you. Sometimes the ways in which He leads will be like the little floor lights along the aisles in the movie theater that guide you to your seat when you arrive after the overhead lights are already dimmed. Even in the darkness, God will make sure to show you where to step.

Your Shepherd knows where the correct paths are. He knows which choices you ought to make. The Shepherd knows which direction you ought to go, and He will make it clear, if you'll let Him take you into the rest mode, and stop being self-sufficient, and stop being determined to figure it all out yourself.

LIKE A MAGNIFYING GLASS

And why will God do this for you? Why will He lead you into His will and show you which way to go?

David tells us: "For His name's sake." Let me remind you what David does *not* say there: "For *my* name's sake."

In the Bible, the concept of *name* is more than just an identifying label. It represents reputation and character. To do something for God's name's sake is to do it for the furtherance of His reputation and for the fame of His character…in other words, for God's glory.

God wants you in the rest position so that when He comes through and shakes things up for you, there won't be any question about who should get the glory and the credit and the praise. God's name will be the only name on the marquee, the only name in the front-page headline, the only author listed on the book cover, because what He does for you He does for His name's sake. He guides you in such a way that He will get glory out of it.

We can make God appear bigger than He otherwise does.

David once expressed it this way: "Oh, magnify the LORD with me, and let us exalt His name together" (Psalm 34:3). So we're like a magnifying glass. Now a magnifying glass doesn't make things bigger; they just appear bigger. We can't actually make God bigger, but in the eyes of others we can make Him appear bigger than He otherwise does. When they see His glory reflecting from us as we live out His will, then others will see things about God that they didn't know before or understand.

COURSE ADJUSTMENT

A car I once owned had a navigational system that for a long time I never used. It was just too much like a computer (in fact, it *was* a computer), and people who know me know that I'm not into computer stuff. So I was stubbornly continuing to find my own way everywhere.

Then one day my son set the system up for me, and punched in where I needed to go that day. He set it all up, and told me the computer would talk to me and tell me where to turn and where to go. So I thought I'd give it a try.

The first thing it told me to do was to back out from my garage. I was shocked. Then it told me how far to continue down the alley to get out onto the street. Step by step it continued giving me every turn to make and the distances for every part of the route, and very soon I was cruising down the freeway. This thing was guiding me all the way, and I was resting. All I had to do was listen to the still small voice of the computer, and it would get me somewhere. The computer had already scoped out the big picture, and it was applying that knowledge to my direction.

It was leading me in the paths that were right.

As I drove along I thought, *This is starting to get fun.* Then, as I continued down the freeway, I decided I would check the computer. When the computer told me to get off at the next exit, I kept going. Immediately after I drove past the exit, the computer screen went blank. It totally shut down. I had beaten the system.

But suddenly the computer popped back on, all by itself, and let me know I would have to take an alternate route. The computer rerouted me. Even though I'd been disobedient and messed up on the first route, even though I had rebelled and chosen my own path, even though I didn't take the way I was supposed to take originally, the computer adjusted to my situation and kept leading me. The computer found me in my disobedience. It found me in my rebellion and created an alternate route, and still got me to the place I was supposed to go.

The Bible calls that grace. Grace is where God meets you, even when you've messed up. He meets you even where you've failed. He meets you even though you've detoured, and He creates an alternate route and still brings you home…so that He will get the glory. He leads us in the right path, always for His name's sake.

Chapter Four

GOD IS MORE
THAN ENOUGH...

to Meet Your Emotional Needs

I hope you're beginning to see that Psalm 23 is more than just a passage for inspirational reading, but rather a functional, fundamental statement of the comprehensive nature of God, and especially of His sufficiency.

And the bottom line: God is more than enough.

In verse 4, David has more good news: He wants you to know that if the Lord is your Shepherd, He'll meet your emotional needs. Look at what David says:

Yea, though I walk through the valley of the
   shadow of death,
I will fear no evil;
   For You are with me;
Your rod and Your staff, they comfort me.

v. 4

David is walking along the way, along the right path in which God has guided him, and yet that path has brought him into a sinister valley, and David must deal with fear.

EMOTIONAL DEFICITS

Fear is a negative emotion, and many today are dominated by such negative feelings because they're living their lives with emotional deficits. Their emotional account is empty. They're waking up every day to more discouragement, more despair, more disappointment, more frustration. The accumulation of the things that bring headache and heartache continues to grow.

There are a lot of reasons for emotional deficits, for these pains of the hearts. For some, it's loneliness, like the little girl who wanted a talking doll because she wanted to press the button and be able to hear somebody say "I love you." Adults just get more expensive toys to battle their loneliness.

Emotional deficits happen when you're drained, when your emotional gas tank is empty and it's only fumes that keep you going. You're dominated by negative feelings, anger, depression, guilt, fear, regret, discouragement. At night you toss and turn because you're overwhelmed with hopelessness, helplessness, and worthlessness.

Some try to deny it, fake it, act like it's not there. Some try to override it. The bars and night clubs are filled with people covering up loneliness, covering up pain, wanting to be distracted, so they don't have to think. Others just go to bed early, so they can go to sleep quicker, and for a few hours at least not have to deal with the disappointments life has sent their way.

To the emotionally drained person the forecast is the same every day: cloudy skies and rain.

Right this moment you may be facing an emotional deficit. Your heart may ache with a debilitating, emotional tug that makes you cry when you don't want to cry, or become angry when you determined not to get angry, or become sad when everybody else is laughing.

David's particular trauma was fear. We see in the Bible that David very often was running for his life. In his later years, even his son wanted to kill him. David had to live much of life under the umbrella of fear. To have fear is to feel you won't make it; it's when you experience a dread that is shredding you.

But for David, as well as for us, to have the Lord as your Shepherd means knowing that He'll meet your emotional needs, no matter how severe your emotional deficit is.

DARK AND GETTING DARKER

David doesn't speak here of going into the valley of death, but into the valley of the *shadow* of death. That's something different from death. The valley looks like death and feels like death, yet it's not death, but only the shadow of it.

When a shepherd led his sheep, sometimes their path went through canyons and valleys so deep that the sunlight was blocked. The shadows were so dark that the sheep would think night had come on, and sheep are scared at night. Nighttime is when foxes and wolves and hyenas come out. It's at nighttime that enemies emerge to devour.

So when the sheep saw the shadows, they thought the worst.

Are you down low in the valley? It may be sunny everywhere else, but down where you are, it's dark. Darkness has come over you, and you feel trapped. You feel emotionally tied to a situation you can't shake; you can't get out of it, no matter what pill you pop, what drink you take, what movie you watch, what advice you get. It's still dark, and it doesn't get any lighter. You're in emotional despair, and you've tried everything you know to get out of it, and nothing has worked.

When God allows you to be in the valley of the shadows, where things are dark and you just want to die, remember that He has given you a gift. When God traps you in the shadows, it's there and only there that you get to see who He really is. God waits while you try all the options, while you pop every pill, drink every drink, talk to every person. And when you finally realize that you've run out of all your options, you're able to discover as never before who He is.

When David finds himself in the valley of the shadow, he's as low as he can get. He isn't on the mountain, where it's easy to feel okay. He's in the valley, and it's a bad valley because it looks like death. Yet he tells us in Psalm 23 that he will not let those circumstances dominate his emotions.

Now don't get me wrong; David doesn't deny the reality of his fear. Trusting God doesn't mean saying, "Oh, I don't ever get frightened," or

In the valley of the shadows, He has given you a gift.

"I never get down or discouraged or frustrated or angry." None of us in honesty can say that. I wish I could tell you that as you get closer to God there'll be no more valleys of the shadow to make you fearful. I wish I could say, "Just be spiritual, and you'll never get discouraged or shaken or terrified." But that isn't true.

David says, however, that in spite of how everything looks in the valley, in spite of how it feels, in spite of the gloom that's crowding in on him like death itself, he isn't going to succumb to fear. Even in that dark abyss he says, "I will fear no evil." Though he feels he's where the foxes and wolves and hyenas could shred him any moment, where it's totally natural to be afraid, he isn't going to yield to the emotional trauma he faces.

ALL YOU HAVE

What made David so strong?

Simple: "You are with me," he told God. His solution to the problem of emotional discouragement was the very presence of God. And that is the key to emotional victory, the key to overcoming emotional traumatization. When you're down and you've run out of human options, that's where God wants you to discover His supernatural presence, the companionship of *His* emotional stability.

When my kids were young and I took them to the haunted house at an amusement park, they wouldn't go through it unless I went with them. And you know how young children, during a thunderstorm late at night, will jump out of their beds and run into their parents' room and jump in bed with them. Doing that doesn't stop the lightning or quiet the thunder, but it changes how they face it. They can fall asleep again, because in the midst of their fear, they know their parents are there with them.

It often takes the darkness of a storm in our lives before we move forward in understanding who God really is. In Mark 4, Jesus and His disciples were in a boat crossing the Sea of Galilee when a huge storm hit them. The disciples were afraid—they were experiencing the valley of the shadow in the middle of the sea.

And where was Jesus? Asleep. What good is a Savior who sleeps on you when you're in a storm? And not only was He asleep, but He was asleep on purpose, because the Bible says His head was "on a pillow" (Mark 4:38). You don't pull out a pillow and lay your head on it unless you intend to go to sleep. So Jesus meant to be sleeping when His followers encountered this storm. Sometimes Jesus will nap on us just when the trial hits.

You know what happens in Mark 4. The disciples wake Jesus up with their shouts. Doesn't He care that they're about to drown? We know that feeling, too; we ask God, *How can You sleep on me during a storm? How can the phone be off the hook at a time like this? How can You not respond to me in my crisis? How can You not answer me in my desperate need?*

After the disciples woke Him up, Jesus stood and rebuked the storm, and said to the sea, "Peace, be still." And the storm-waves and the storm-wind submitted immediately to His authority, and "there was a great calm" (v. 39). Then Jesus turned to the disciples and said, "Why are you so fearful? How is it that you have no faith?" (v. 40).

How did the disciples respond to all this? "They *feared exceedingly,* and said to one another, '*Who can this be,* that even the wind and the sea obey Him!'" (v. 41). They had been scared of the storm, but when they saw Who was bigger than the storm, they became terrified even more. In that tempest they had seen who God is.

When He's all you have, He's all you need.

And for us also, it's in the midst of life's storm that God lets us glimpse Him and worship Him as we never can otherwise. God will let you get in an emotional storm because He wants to hear you say what David said: "Whenever I am afraid, I will trust in You. In God (I will praise His word), in God I have put my trust; I will not fear" (Psalm 56:3–4). When God has you in the shadows and you see no way out, He has taken you there for a purpose, and that purpose is entirely about *your view of Him.*

It's only when you realize He's all you have that you discover He's all you need—when all other options have run out, and you must throw yourself on Him if you're to make it even one step further.

HIS ROD OF POWER

What do you receive when the presence of God walks with you in the valley to drive away your fears?

David tells us: "Your rod and Your staff, they comfort me."

When there's a traffic accident, two agencies rush to the scene to give emergency assistance: police and paramedics. Because of the crisis, those two units are called. And David says God has two units available to you in a crisis, His rod and His staff.

Every shepherd carried a rod that was like a club he used to beat away any creature that attacked the sheep. It was a weapon of power, and God's rod represents His power, His awesome power to address anything that would attack you. "Power belongs to God," David said (Psalm 62:11).

There are plenty of earthly authorities who are powerful, but they can only go so far; God alone is *all*-powerful. I love it when I see God overrule the rulers, the people who think they have all the power and who flaunt what power they do have, or their education, or their money, or their status, or their notoriety. Everybody else is bowing at their feet; but God still stands up tall to let them know, "There is no God but Me."

In His will, you're safer than anywhere else you could be.

If you're where God wants you, even if it's in the storm, you're safer than anywhere else you could be. The prophet Daniel was safe and at peace in the lion's den, while the king in his palace stayed awake all that night with worry. You're safer with God in a bad place than you are without Him in what you think is a good place.

I had to learn this from my father, who still lives in the ghetto. I've been trying for years to get him to move, but he won't. I went to visit him recently and as we sat on the porch, we saw drug deals going on down the street, and two women started fighting in the middle of the street like cats and dogs. It was another normal day in that neighborhood.

"Daddy," I said, "why won't you move? This is not a safe place."

"Boy," he answered (he still calls me that); "boy, let me explain something. The same God who got you out of this neighborhood, and the same God that got your brothers and sister out of this neighborhood, is the very same God that I've got with me right now. If God tells me to move, I'll move. But He has me at peace right where I am, and if I'm in His will, I'm as safe here in the ghetto as anybody out in the suburbs." Daddy understands the rod of God.

HIS STAFF OF GRACE

When David insists, "I will not fear," it's not only because of God's rod, God's power, but also because of His staff—which represents God's grace.

The shepherd would use his crook-topped staff to reach in and pull out a sheep from the brambles where it was caught. The staff was the tool to untrap the sheep.

Have you ever been trapped? Have you ever been caught in something you couldn't get delivered from? God not only has power, but He has grace, and grace is when God reaches in to your caughtness, to your stuck-ness, and pulls you out. God reaches in to deliver you from the situation you've gotten yourself caught in.

Do you really understand grace? Grace is where God gives you what you don't deserve. Grace is where God is good when you are bad. Grace is where He is kind while you are unkind. Grace is where He is loving when you don't deserve to be loved. He reaches in anyway and delivers you. He blesses you anyway. He takes care of you anyway. That's God's grace.

I've heard they have a new product for washing machines that keeps colored clothing from bleeding and discoloring other clothes in the same washload. It's a little absorbent sheet that you throw in the washer, and it soaks up any color that bleeds from the clothes while the washer is tumbling and spinning and going through the motions.

Sometimes life tumbles you around. And the enemy is out there to bleed and discolor you, disfigure you and destroy you, and you're spinning and turning and twisting and tumbling. But God's presence enters that environment, and He keeps the evil one from having the last say-so in your life.

That's what God does. That's why the Bible says we're to be "looking unto Jesus, the author and finisher of our faith" (Hebrews 12:2).

The Bible says that "perfect love casts out fear" (1 John

4:18). When you know how much God loves you, when you know how much God cares for you, when you know how much He thinks about you, when you know how valued you are…it will overrule any emotion that seeks to tear you down.

THE FINAL WORD

Yes, I would love to be able to tell you that by being a good Christian, you won't get disheartened, and your relationships will go as smoothly as you ever dreamed, and your finances will be doubled tomorrow; just be a fine Christian and it will all be yours—but you and I know life doesn't work like that. There are good days and bad days. Sometimes living is hell and sometimes living is heaven. Sometimes you're on the mountain and sometimes you're in the valley.

David wants you to know that there will be emotional highs and there will be the shadows of death. But even in those seasons of darkest shadow, we don't have to let our emotions have the final word; we can let our God have the final Word.

So don't you quit on Him. Don't throw in the towel. You are loved too much for that. And God in His love for you has a plan and a purpose for your time in the valley.

God can meet you where you are, and give you sunshine. He can meet you where you are, and give you joy. He can meet you where you are, and give you peace.

Your God is bigger than your need.

Chapter Five

GOD IS MORE
THAN ENOUGH...

to Meet Your Physical Needs

Here's something else David wants you to know: If the Lord is your Shepherd, He'll meet your *physical* needs. God, as your good Shepherd, is a perfect provider.

David says,

> You prepare a table before me in the
> presence of my enemies;
> You anoint my head with oil;
> My cup runs over.

v. 5

Who Sets Your Table?

To "prepare a table" is to provide a meal. It has to do with meeting our most basic, substantive physical needs. And this, David says, is what the Lord our Shepherd does for us.

I can't cook, and I have no interest in learning. I have no inclinations toward the kitchen. I even burn water when I boil it. It's a pretty bad situation.

And because I don't cook, whatever meals I eat have to be prepared by somebody else. I don't have to get all involved in it, which is fine with me. I simply come to a table that's already been prepared. I don't worry about the grocery list or about the shopping. I don't get concerned about the seasonings, or about which pot and which pan and which utensils to use. I don't deal with any of that. I smell the food while it's cooking, and when it's done I eat it; but I have that privilege only because somebody else has taken responsibility for getting it all ready. Someone else has prepared a table before me.

God alone sets the table.

Fundamental to our understanding of God as our Shepherd is the realization that the Lord Himself is the ultimate Preparer of our table. God alone is the Source of all our provisions. For some reason, we often don't understand this. *We* want to take credit for being the source of our provisions. Maybe it's because of our knowledge, our education, our talent, our skill—but somehow, we think we're the supplier.

David says to God, *"You* prepare a table before me." David understands that God alone grants the supply. Now there usually are interim steps involved before God's provision gets to you, but without God as the source, you would never see it. When it comes to the food on your table, behind the intermediaries—the grocery store and the merchandiser and the distributor and the packager and the farmer—behind them all are the seeds and the soil and the sun and the rain that come ultimately and only from God. If God doesn't provide, we don't eat, because there's nothing to eat.

God is the starting point. He can use as many vehicles and intermediaries as He wishes, and each one is important and significant. But don't confuse them with the Source. Remember who the true Provider is.

That's why every time you come to the table, it's appropriate to "say grace"—to offer thanksgiving to God. When somebody sets something for your enjoyment and nourishment in front of you, common courtesy alone would stipulate that you're to respond by saying, "Thank you," right? It's entirely fitting and proper to express your gratitude.

But when we ungratefully forget the Source and treat

the intermediaries as if they're the source, we turn them into a god. We're literally worshiping the creature rather than the Creator when we fail to thankfully view God as the starting point.

Ultimate Source

Years ago when my son was young, I was teaching him about giving. He had an allowance of two dollars, and I required that he give ten percent of that to the Lord. He was bothered about that twenty cents he had to give up; he had an attitude about it. It seemed to him that he was being cheating out of that twenty cents.

So I asked him, "Where did you get the two dollars from?"

"Well, I got it from you."

"And where did I get the money to give you the two dollars?"

"You got it from your salary, from your job."

"And how was I able to get a salary from my job?"

"Well, people work, and they give money to the church."

"Yes, that's absolutely right. So how do they get the money to give?"

"They work at their jobs."

And we kept tracing it back. We looked at the different jobs people have, and going back further and further we discovered that every job on our planet depends on raw materials. In fact, we wouldn't even have currency to spend if we didn't have the paper it's printed on.

"So," I asked my son, "where do the raw materials come from that provide the opportunity to produce the productivity that creates the jobs, so people can be paid, so they can then give, so I can have a salary, so you can get your two dollars?"

God alone is

the Source.

"From God, I guess," he answered. And I think that week he put thirty cents in the collection plate.

So God alone is the Source, and everybody else is an intermediary. It's ultimately God, and nobody else, who sets the table and provides for our needs.

WHAT IS A NEED?

Remember God's promise? "And my God shall supply all your need according to His riches in glory by Christ Jesus" (Philippians 4:19). But don't misread that; Paul isn't saying that God will supply all your *wants* or all your *desires;* he's saying God will supply all that you truly need.

But what is a need? A true need is a life essential. Physically, it has to do with food, with clothes, with shelter. These things are essentials to human life. And these are what God will never fail to supply.

What is a want? A want is like a life essential that's been upgraded. It's not just clothing we're after; we want designer brands. And what is a desire? A desire is a want upgrade: Not only would you like a car, but you'd like a Rolls-Royce Phantom.

There's nothing wrong with wants or desires. It's okay to have them. But desires and wants are different from a need, and they don't carry the same promise from God.

God shall supply all your *needs;* He'll also supply *some* of your wants, and from time to time He'll even give you a few of your desires.

But again remember this: The Bible tells us that when He provides even basic needs, you're to give thanks. If you have a roof over your head and clothes on your back and food in your stomach, give thanks. Why should God give you your wants when you haven't even thanked Him for meeting your basic needs?

I once had a dog—emphasis on "had." His name was Solomon, and he ate from a bowl on the floor of the laundry room. One day as he was feeding, I was in the laundry room and I dropped something on the floor next to his bowl. As I bent down to get it, Solomon growled and snapped at me. He thought I was getting too close to his food.

Solomon had an attitude.

Now, I had been feeding that dog for years. I was Solomon's provider. He neither made that bowl he ate from, nor did he buy it—I bought it for him. I also bought his watering bowl, and when it was empty, I took it to the sink and brought it back full. I cleaned up the messes Solomon made in my house. And when Solomon had to go out late at night or early in the morning to relieve himself, I got up to open the door for him.

I was that dog's provider…but he failed to remember that. And now Solomon no longer lives in my house.

Are you failing to remember who your provider is? Or are you giving Him thanks?

ENEMIES LOOKING ON

David tells us that God prepares His table for us regardless of the surrounding circumstances. He does it even with our enemies looking on.

The shepherd prepares the table for the sheep even with the foxes and hyenas and wolves up in the hills surveying the scene, wishing they could have those sheep they see—but they can't, because the shepherd is there with his rod and staff.

"In the presence of enemies," David says. What is an enemy? An enemy is anything that threatens our sustenance or security. An enemy is anything that can get in the way of needs being met, anything that truly threatens us and our physical requirements and well-being. We won't be traveling through life without facing these threats, but God still knows how to prepare tables even when we face them.

God is not subject to the economy. God is not subject to the stock market. God is not subject to the jobless rate. God isn't subject to any circumstances. In the midst of bad times He still knows how to set good tables within sight of our enemies—in the presence of inflation or depression or recession or a bad supervisor or a pink slip.

God is not subject to the economy.

Whatever might be blocking the provision of your physical needs, God knows how to move that obstacle out of the way. God know how to provide in the presence of our enemies because He's bigger than our enemies.

A half century ago, in some locations across the American South where black students tried to become the first of their race to enroll in public schools and universities, local and state officials sometimes would stand in the schoolhouse door to prevent desegregation. But repeatedly they were confronted by federal marshals or National Guard troops or officials from the U.S. Department of Justice, and forced to step aside and allow these students to exercise their rights. Why did the opponents of liberty and racial equality have to step aside? Because someone bigger showed up.

Whatever might be blocking your provision, when God shows up, He can move it out of the way.

A woman in our church was being harassed at work by her supervisor, who didn't like her because she was a Christian. "This is driving me crazy," she told us. "I know this is the job I'm supposed to be in, but I can't work for this man anymore. And I need God to do something."

So we prayed that God would do something soon.

A week later her supervisor's boss called her in and told her they didn't like the supervisor's performance; they had fired him, and promoted her to his job. So God provided—right in the presence of her enemies.

SUPER-SIZE

David also tells us this about the Lord who sets our table: "You anoint my head with oil."

In the Scriptures, the concept of anointing is associated most with the Holy Spirit and with joy. This is what keeps the irritations and vexations of life from overwhelming us.

It's a wonderful thing to see a saint experiencing the joy of the Lord while going through a difficult time physically. The joy of the Lord doesn't necessarily remove the difficulty or the pain, but it's the role of the Holy Spirit to be our Comforter. He soothes the wound, to bring healing and comfort in the midst of the pain.

God knows how to soothe you with His anointing. He's your personal Physician, either administering a solution to the problem, or giving you a peace that can sustain you in middle of it.

David also says, "My cup overflows." He knows that even when there are enemies in sight, and the valleys are full of shadows, his cup is full and overflowing, the liquid lapping over the brim. And that means, *"I have more than enough."* God knows how to overflow our situation, right where we are.

It's like the times Jesus fed the multitudes by multiplying a tiny amount of loaves and fishes, and on each occasion there were several basketfuls of leftovers. The Lord had provided those thousands of people with more than enough. Their cups ran over.

It's also like when Jesus told Peter to go out into the

deep and cast his nets, after he'd fished all night and caught nothing. Peter obeyed, and their catch that morning was enough to rip their nets and almost caused their boat to swamp. That's overflowing.

God knows how to super-size His provision for every situation. He gives more than enough.

Now sometimes He'll super-size His provision of joy for you when there are no great difficulties in your situation; but He'll especially super-size His provision in the middle of a conflict, a challenge, a hardship, and that's when you know He's real, because you know that in such unwelcome circumstances there's no natural explanation for why you're feeling like this—why you're experiencing joy and fullness.

God knows how to super-size His provision.

The Bible says God has surplus grace—"And God is able to make all grace abound toward you, that you, always having all sufficiency in all things, may have an abundance for every good work" (2 Corinthians 9:8). For every situation, for all times, in everything, God has an abundance of grace for us.

He also has a surplus of hope for you—He's the "God of hope" who saturates you with joy and peace, "so that you may overflow with hope by the power of the Holy Spirit" (Romans 15:13, NIV).

He gives a surplus of joy—He causes you to "rejoice with joy inexpressible and full of glory" (1 Peter 1:8).

And He provides a surplus of peace—He gives "the peace of God, which surpasses all understanding" (Philippians 4:7).

Our God "is able to do exceedingly abundantly above all that we ask or think, according to the power that works in us" (Ephesians 3:20). He is able to do this because within Himself He has more than enough to meet your every need.

Whenever God allows you to get trapped in an inconvenient situation—like losing a job—it's only to help move you up to the next level of trust in His provision. He wants you to experience His surplus goodness as you look to Him as your major provider.

WHEN GOD DOES NOT SUPPLY

There are only two times in our lives when God won't meet our physical needs.

The first is when He's trying to strip us of our self-sufficiency, when we're still too independent. So He withholds His provision as He works to break us.

And the second time is when it's our time to go home. When that moment comes, He won't heal or sustain our body because it's time to leave that body, and to instead enter His presence.

But apart from those two occasions, we'll always be able to affirm what David testified: "I have never seen the righteous forsaken or their children begging bread" (Psalm 37:25, NIV). Because God is more than faithful to meet our every physical need.

Chapter Six

GOD IS MORE
THAN ENOUGH...
to *Meet Your Eternal Needs*

We've come to the closing line of Psalm 23, and David begins it with the word *surely.* He doesn't lead off with *maybe;* he doesn't use *perhaps* or *possibly;* and he doesn't start with *hopefully.* He says, "Surely"—a biblical term of certainty.

There's no guesswork for David on this, no doubts, no wondering, no hesitation, no question marks. He says, "Surely"—sure enough, absolutely, without a doubt.

And what is David so sure about? He's confident that if the Lord is our Shepherd, He'll meet all our *eternal* needs:

> Surely goodness and mercy shall follow me
>   All the days of my life;
> And I will dwell in the house of
>   the LORD forever.

v. 6

SURE AND SECURE

Remember again that this isn't a psalm about problemless circumstances. David has needed his soul restored; he has needed direction; he's faced fear and needed the assurance of the Lord's presence.

And in this crucible of neediness, David has learned some lessons:

—Where the grass is greenest, that's where God takes me and makes me lie down. Where the water is most quiet, He leads me. And there He gives me back the spiritual energy I've lost.

—When I'm confused and unsure what I ought to do, my Shepherd guides me forward in the paths that are right.

He does this for one reason only: so He can get the credit: "For His name's sake."

—When I'm terrified by my circumstances, and down as low into darkness as I think I could possibly go, He shows up. He brings a rod and a staff (His power and His grace), and I feel better. They comfort me.

— It really doesn't matter how bad my external circumstances seem to be, because He still knows how to lay a table in the presence of the worst scenarios conceivable. He even bestows gladness and peace and rest upon me as He anoints and massages my head. I can jump for joy because I'm so overflowing with gladness, as my cup runs over.

Out of these lessons, David goes on to say, "Surely." And so can we. In the midst of our confusion, discouragement, and depression, we can be *sure*, and that means we can be *secure*.

David says, "Surely," and so can we.

At the heart of rightly understanding this psalm is realizing that when the Lord is your Shepherd, He's *for* you. "This I know," David says in another psalm, "that God is for me" (56:9, NASB). God has adopted you, and not only that, He's obsessed with you. He can't get you off His mind once you become part of His family. You're part of His passion—and there's security in that.

WHATEVER IS NECESSARY

I was raised poor, but I always knew I was loved. I knew my parents would go to whatever extent necessary to meet our needs as their children.

I don't eat fish today, and let me tell you why. When I was about ten or twelve years old, my father was out of work because all the longshoremen in Baltimore harbor were on strike. But he had to feed his family, so he went fishing, and he caught herring.

Herring, in case you didn't know, are little fish that have a million bones, and they're tiny bones. And my father caught them not with a rod but with a net, so over time he brought home thousands of herring to feed his family. I think we had herring and eggs for breakfast, herring sandwiches for lunch, fried herring for dinner, and herring pudding for dessert. It was all we had.

From that I developed a hatred for fish, because every time I see fish, I see herring. But at least I learned the certainty that my daddy was going to feed us. He loved his family and was tenaciously committed to caring for us, and I never worried about that.

Why are we sometimes insecure? Because we stop remembering how much our Daddy in heaven loves us.

YOUR INSURANCE POLICY

Psalm 23 is saying that God is your insurance policy.

Someone might respond, "With my other insurance policies, I have to keep the premiums up; if I don't, I'm not insured anymore. So what do I have to do to keep God's policy in effect? Do I need to pay the premium of church attendance? Do I need to pay the premium of being a nice person? Do I need to pay the premium of giving my tithes and offerings?"

No—and the mere fact that someone thinks that way is evidence he doesn't understand God's commitment to us.

One day at lunch when I was in the eighth grade, a boy stole a piece of chicken out of my plate, and a fight was on! I got suspended from school because of it, and they had to call my father at his job to come get me. He worked by the hour, which meant he had to punch out on the time clock to come and learn why his son had been kicked out of school.

He found me sitting in the principal's office, where the principal explained the situation to him. My father looked at me, then he looked at the principal, and he said, "Sir, you will never, ever, ever"—each time he said "ever," I sank lower in my chair— "*ever* have to worry about my son ever being suspended from school ever again."

Daddy was ticked off with me. As we walked out of the

school he told me, "Do you know how much this visit is costing me? And I'm taking the payment out on you."

And yet, even though I got a whipping for that, my father still continued to feed me. He still clothed me. There was still a roof over my head. I had done something to irritate him, but he was still my daddy. He was tenaciously committed to me, and I didn't have to earn that commitment.

God Himself has paid the premium.

So if the Lord is your Shepherd, is there a premium to pay for His insurance?

Yes there is, but let me tell you how committed God is to you. He's so committed to you that He Himself has picked up the payment of the premium. It's been paid and written in blood, the blood of His Son, Jesus Christ. The premium is covered, so you never have to pay it. That's how much God is committed to you and obsessed with you.

THE COVERAGE TERMS

So how long does this insurance coverage stay in effect?

I'll tell you: It secures you throughout time (which is now), and it secures you for all eternity.

First David says, "Surely goodness and mercy shall follow me *all the days of my life."* All your time is covered—every day of your earthly existence, from now until you die. God is so committed to you that even though you might walk away from Him, He's never going to walk away from you.

As your Good Shepherd leads you throughout your days here on earth, His goodness and mercy will follow you, like good sheepdogs running along behind. They've got your backside covered, so that even if you wander, you can't go too far. The Shepherd's faithful dogs, goodness and mercy, will sniff you out and track you down and steer you back.

GOODNESS AND MERCY

What does "goodness" represent? Goodness includes all the benefits that accrue from God to you, all His beneficial acts of kindness toward you.

If you were to list on a piece of paper all the manifestations of God's goodness toward you, and you were serious and undistracted, you would be writing for days at least. You're alive and breathing only because you're borrowing air on loan. You're moving and functioning only because of the

His good things surround you in every way possible.

way the parts in your body have been constructed to work, according to the creative biological systems that God set up. His good things literally surround you in every way possible.

David sang to the Lord, "Oh, how great is Your goodness, which You have laid up for those who fear You, which You have prepared for those who trust in You" (Psalm 31:19). And Psalm 84:11 tells us, "No good thing will He withhold from those who walk uprightly."

Besides goodness, the other sheepdog is mercy, or, as the New American Standard Bible translates it, "lovingkindness." The Hebrew term there is *hesed,* one of the richest and most encouraging words in the Hebrew language. *Hesed* speaks of the Lord's loyal commitment to you. He's committed to you unconditionally. He's not committed to you *if;* He's committed to you *because* He's committed to you. On your best day, He's committed to you; on your worst day, He's committed to you.

Any loving parent understands this. You're committed to your child, not to everything your child does. He may be your bad son, but he's still your son; she may be your arrogant daughter, but she's still your daughter. They're yours, and that's why you love them even when you don't like them, because they're yours.

God loves you because you're you. It's true that He wants you to change some of your ways and do some things differently, but when you do, it won't make Him love you any more than He already does. And no matter how far short you fall of the desirable improvements, it can't make Him love you less. He loves you because He loves you.

Oh, what a way to live, knowing with absolute certainty that His goodness and His loyal love will stick with me for the rest of my life!

TRUE HOME

And when my life on earth is over, I'll have just gotten started with the blessings, for I will dwell in the Lord's house forever, just as David says.

That word *dwell* means to be at home. When you leave this world and go to be with the Lord, because you've accepted Jesus Christ as your Savior, only then will you finally be home. Which means you're *not* home now.

The love of God for some of us isn't real because we've tried to make this earth our home. But when we treat this life and this world like home, we give it a position it was never meant to have, and we'll only be confused and miserable. Only when we have the right view of our true home will we have the right view of *here*.

That's why, when you understand your true home, death is never a period; instead it's a conjunction. Less than one second after the Christian dies, he or she is ushered into the presence of God. They aren't even dead long enough to know they died. That's why Christians need not be afraid to die, because they're never going to expire; they're going to transfer, quicker than they can blink, from one dimension to another. They'll go instantly from living in this time, where goodness and mercy follow us all the days of our lives, to dwelling forever in the house of the Lord. *Bam,* just like that, they'll be home.

Only the right view of home gives us the right view of here.

If we let a perspective of our true home dominate us here, then here will be much more tolerable. We can tolerate here because we know that here isn't all there is. And God will help us sense this more and more.

Most of us will not die suddenly, with a heart attack or stroke or in a car crash; for most of us, death will come more gradually as our bodies wear down over time. You'll feel your body deteriorating and wasting away, and you'll know you're closing in on death. Then God will put you in the transition mode, as He creates a scenario that makes you want to be home more than you want to stay here.

In that season He'll make heaven look much more

appealing than earth, so that you'll be thinking, *I wish God would just hurry and take me home.* God will let you get a little preview into glory, and let you see your Savior waiting to welcome You. When you glimpse those arms open wide, you'll want the trip to hurry up and take place.

THE SHORELINE IN SIGHT

Florence Chadwick was the first woman to swim the English Channel, and she later took on the challenge of swimming the twenty-one miles from Catalina Island to the shoreline of California. But after sixteen hours in the fog-enshrouded Pacific waters, she quit, exhausted and discouraged. Soon after climbing into the boat and heading for shore, she got a clear view of the coast she was aiming for—it was only a half mile from where she'd stopped swimming. You can imagine her disappointment.

Two months later she tried it again, and this time she made it in record time. It was another foggy day; she still couldn't see that far in front of her; she was in the same depressing circumstances she'd been in before. But this time she didn't quit.

Later she explained what made the difference: With every stroke she took, she had a picture of the shoreline in her head. Each time she began to get discouraged, she pulled up that picture in her thoughts. Though her external circumstances were the same as before, her internal vision was dramatically different.

If you keep in mind how much God loves you, and if you keep in mind the shoreline of your future, you'll allow Him and His two guard dogs, goodness and lovingkindness, to keep you pressing forward even when you want to quit. You'll know that even though your circumstances are bad, your God is good, heaven is your home, and He is with you all the way.

And you'll know without a doubt that your Father loves you—not "maybe" or "perhaps," but *surely.*

The publisher and author would love to hear your comments about this book. *Please contact us at:* www.bigchangemoments.com

THE URBAN ALTERNATIVE

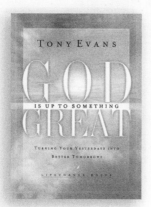

GOD IS UP TO SOMETHING GREAT

Turning Your Yesterdays into Better Tomorrows

Are you living with regrets? Discover the positives of your past. Tony Evans shows how God means to use your experiences—good, bad, and ugly—to lead you toward your purpose.

ISBN 1-59052-038-6

THE FIRE THAT IGNITES

Living in the Power of the Holy Spirit

Dr. Evans shows how the power of the Spirit brings wisdom, freedom, and joy—and how holy habits can keep you "plugged in" to the eternal source of spiritual power.

ISBN 1-59052-083-1

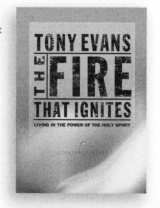

BIG CHANGE

TRUE FREEDOM
The Liberating Power of Prayer
OLIVER NORTH & BRIAN SMITH
ISBN 1-59052-363-6

THE PRAYER MATRIX
Plugging in to the Unseen Reality
DAVID JEREMIAH ISBN 1-59052-181-1
(Available February 2004)

AFTER YOU'VE BLOWN IT
Reconnecting with God and Others
ERWIN LUTZER ISBN 1-59052-334-2
(Available March 2004)

GOD IS MORE THAN ENOUGH
TONY EVANS ISBN 1-59052-337-7

THE FIRE THAT IGNITES
Living in the Power of the Holy Spirit
TONY EVANS ISBN 1-59052-083-1

GOD IS UP TO SOMETHING GREAT
Turning Your Yesterdays into
Better Tomorrows
TONY EVANS ISBN 1-59052-038-6

HOW GOOD IS GOOD ENOUGH?
ANDY STANLEY ISBN 1-59052-274-5

THE AIR I BREATHE
Worship as a Way of Life
LOUIE GIGLIO ISBN 1-59052-153-6

WHAT'S SO SPIRITUAL ABOUT YOUR GIFTS?
HENRY BLACKABY ISBN 1-59052-344-X
(Available April 2004)

**WHAT THE SPIRIT IS SAYING
TO THE CHURCHES**
HENRY BLACKABY ISBN 1-59052-036-X

**WHAT THE SPIRIT IS SAYING TO THE
CHURCHES BIBLE STUDY**
ISBN 1-59052-216-8

A LITTLE POT OF OIL
A Life Overflowing
JILL BRISCOE ISBN 1-59052-234-6

IN THE SECRET PLACE
For God and You Alone
J. OTIS LEDBETTER ISBN 1-59052-252-4

OUR JEALOUS GOD
Love That Won't Let Me Go
BILL GOTHARD ISBN 1-59052-225-7

THE POWER OF CRYING OUT
When Prayer Becomes Mighty
BILL GOTHARD ISBN 1-59052-037-8

WRESTLING WITH GOD
Prayer That Never Gives Up
GREG LAURIE ISBN 1-59052-044-0

SIMPLY JESUS
Experiencing the One Your Heart Longs For
JOSEPH M. STOWELL ISBN 1-57673-856-6

SMALL BOOKS
BIG CHANGE

BIG CHANGE

GROWING A SPIRITUALLY STRONG FAMILY
Family First Series, #1
DENNIS & BARBARA RAINEY
ISBN 1-57673-778-0

TWO HEARTS PRAYING AS ONE
Family First Series, #2
DENNIS & BARBARA RAINEY
ISBN 1-59052-035-1

PRESSURE PROOF YOUR MARRIAGE
Family First Series, #3
DENNIS & BARBARA RAINEY
ISBN 1-59052-211-7

THE PURITY PRINCIPLE
God's Safeguards for Life's Dangerous Trails
RANDY ALCORN ISBN 1-59052-195-1

THE GRACE AND TRUTH PARADOX
Responding with Christlike Balance
RANDY ALCORN ISBN 1-59052-065-3

THE TREASURE PRINCIPLE
Discovering the Secret of Joyful Giving
RANDY ALCORN ISBN 1-57673-780-2

THE TREASURE PRINCIPLE BIBLE STUDY
ISBN 1-59052-187-0

THE HEART OF A TENDER WARRIOR
Becoming a Man of Purpose
STU WEBER ISBN 1-59052-039-4

SIX STEPS TO SPIRITUAL REVIVAL
God's Awesome Power in Your Life
PAT ROBERTSON ISBN 1-59052-055-6

CERTAIN PEACE IN UNCERTAIN TIMES
Embracing Prayer in an Anxious Age
SHIRLEY DOBSON ISBN 1-57673-937-6

THE CROSS CENTERED LIFE
Experiencing the Power of the Gospel
C. J. MAHANEY ISBN 1-59052-045-9

THE DANGEROUS DUTY OF DELIGHT
The Glorified God and the
Satisfied Soul
JOHN PIPER ISBN 1-57673-883-3

RIGHT WITH GOD
Loving Instruction from the
Father's Heart
RON MEHL ISBN 1-59052-186-2

A PRAYER THAT MOVES HEAVEN
Comfort and Hope for Life's Most
Difficult Moments
RON MEHL ISBN 1-57673-885-X

THE LOTUS AND THE CROSS
Jesus Talks with Buddha
RAVI ZACHARIAS ISBN 1-57673-854-X

SENSE AND SENSUALITY
Jesus Talks with Oscar Wilde
RAVI ZACHARIAS ISBN 1-59052-014-9

SMALL BOOKS
BIG CHANGE™